New Piano Course

For Adults and Older Children

Will Waitt has been teaching, performing and composing piano music for over 30 years. This has given him in-depth knowledge and experience about all aspects of learning the piano.

This book can offer anyone who wants to play the piano a unique and easy to follow method. It will give you the building blocks of musical knowledge and technique and allow you to improve your playing from beginner to reciting fully fledged pieces.

After mastering and understanding each of the 25 stages you will be able to recite well known and original piano music and be on your way to becoming a confident and fluent player.

CONTENTS

KNOWING THE KEYBOARD

Look at the keyboard and notice how the black notes are arranged in groups of 2 and then 3 all along the keyboard.

The note C is found to the left of a group of 2 black keys:

C

Now, on the keyboard, follow the alphabet from C to G ascending, (to the right) on the white notes of the keyboard. Only the first 7 letters of the alphabet are used, so at G the next note up on the keyboard is A, then B, etc.

Likewise, descend from C (left) and follow the alphabet in reverse; B, A, then G and F etc.

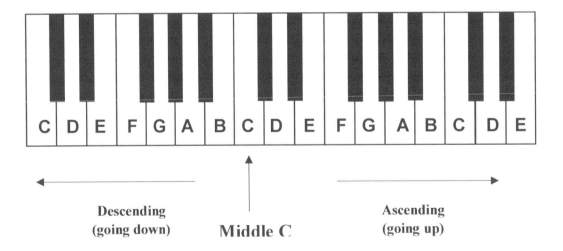

Descending
(going down)

Middle C

Ascending
(going up)

Middle C is the most central C on the piano or keyboard. Find this note and think of the letter names of the white notes and their relationship with the black keys. For example, F can be found just to the left of a group of 3 black keys.

Also play any note at random, then work out its letter name. The more familiar you get with the keyboard at this stage, the easier everything will be in the future.

FINGER NUMBERS AND HAND POSITIONS

Think of each hand as a mirror copy of the other. Start with thumbs as first fingers or 1's, then count out to little fingers (5's).

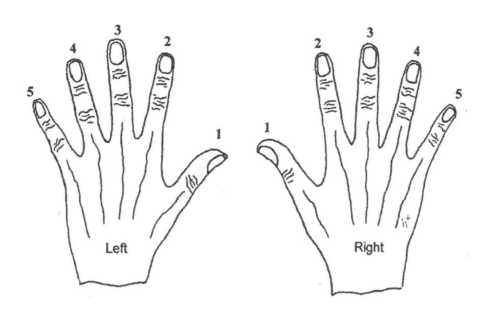

Sit comfortably at the piano with middle C directly in front of you and place your right hand thumb (1) on that key. The second finger (2) on D, third on E until all five fingers are touching five adjacent white keys (C position).

It is very important for the arm to feel as relaxed as possible. Try resting your right hand (R.H) on a table, palm down with the fingers slightly bent. Raise your arm and wrist a little so the top of the hand is parallel to the table top. Hold this position for 20 seconds trying not to feel any tension, then do the same with the left hand (L.H).

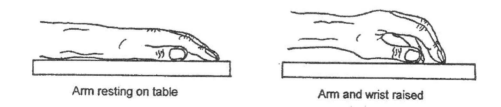

Arm resting on table   Arm and wrist raised

Now, transfer this position back to the keyboard and you're ready to play.

USING ALL 5 FINGERS IN RIGHT HAND

First play all the notes of C position ascending and descending starting from middle C.

Note: the numbers above and below the notes are the finger numbers.

R. H. (Right Hand)

1	2	3	4	5	4	3	2	1
C	D	E	F	G	F	E	D	C

Keep fingers close to the keys and the arm and hand as tension free as possible. Play the notes at a slow, even pace and keep legato; a musical term for smooth.

Now try this familiar tune using the same hand position.

FRÈRE JACQUES

1	2	3	1		1	2	3	1		3	4	5		3	4	5
C	D	E	C		C	D	E	C		E	F	G*		E	F	G*

1	2	3	1		1	2	3	1		3	2	1		3	2	1
C	D	E	C		C	D	E	C		E	D	C*		E	D	C*

* All the notes should be played at the same steady beat except the notes marked with an asterisk. These should be held for 2 beats, (twice as long).

USING ALL 5 FINGERS IN LEFT HAND

Play all the notes in the left hand, starting with fingers on the C below middle C.

L. H. (Left Hand)	C	D	E	F	G	F	E	D	C
	5	4	3	2	1	2	3	4	5

Just like the right hand, keep your left hand and arm relaxed, and play only with your fingers.

Here is the first piece for the left hand.

ODE TO JOY

E	E	F	G	G	F	E	D	C	C	D	E	E	D	D *
3	3	2	1	1	2	3	4	5	5	4	3	3	4	4
	2									2				

E	E	F	G	G	F	E	D	C	C	D	E	F	G	G *
3	3	2	1	1	2	3	4	5	5	4	3	2	1	1
	2									2				

* As with Frère Jacques, all the notes should be played at the same speed, except those marked with an asterisk which you hold for 2 beats each.

Note: As you play these pieces, look at the keyboard and try to memorise where all 5 keys are. (See Stage 1).

TIMING

All music has a beat or pulse moving through it. The basic one-beat note is called a "crotchet" or quarter note. Four of these make up one bar or measure, and look solid black with a stem. (♩)

If the notes are not filled in they would have the value of 2 beats each. They are minims or half notes. (♩)

Play this rhythm on middle C with the right hand thumb. Count 4 beats each bar.

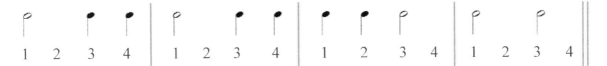

Now play this rhythm on middle C with the left hand thumb.

Use all 5 fingers in the right hand for this next piece.

MELODY IN C

Finger numbers

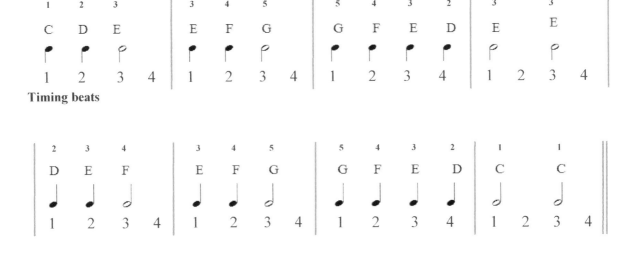

Timing beats

Stage 4 (cont.)

When a note is held for a whole bar (4 beats), it looks like a minim without the stem and is called a semibreve or whole note (o).

Play this in C position in the L. H. (see page 4).

MERRILY WE ROLL ALONG

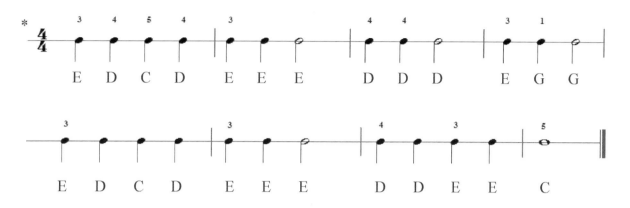

* This is called a time-signature and tells the player that each bar consists of 4 crotchet beats. While this is the most common time signature, 2, 3, or even 5 beats a bar can be used.

Play this in C position R. H.

LIGHTLY ROW

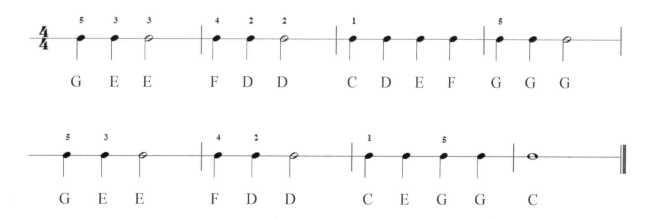

Once you feel familiar with the notes, count the beats (1, 2, 3, 4) in every bar as you play.

READING MUSIC

All notes are written on a stave which consists of 5 lines and 4 spaces.

Notes are written either in the spaces (those without lines running through them):

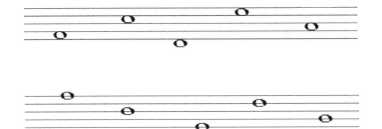

or on the lines:

The upper half of the piano, (from about middle C) is written in the treble clef;

Note: music written in this clef is nearly always played with the right hand.

The lower half of the keyboard is called the bass clef; and is generally played with the left hand.

Note: the nearer the top of the stave a note is written, the higher up the keyboard it is played.

In this example, the first note is the highest, the last note the lowest.

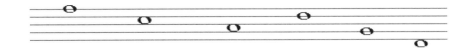

Sometimes notes have to be written below or above the stave, (e.g. middle C).

The line drawn through this note is called a ledger line.

When notes are adjacent to each other on the keyboard they are also written in adjacent lines and spaces on the stave.

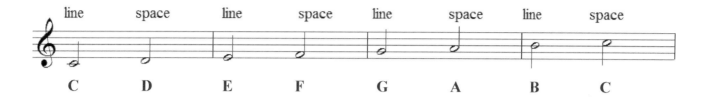

If you see a line note next to another line note, you skip or miss out one note on the keyboard.

This will also occur when moving from space note to space note.

Stage 5 (cont.)

A method to remember the notes on the stave is to match the first letter of these little sayings with the notes, working up from the lowest line or space.

First the treble clef space notes:

F   A   C   E

Now the treble clef line notes:

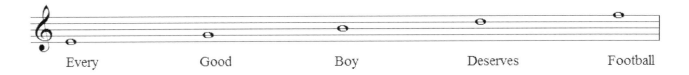

Every   Good   Boy   Deserves   Football

Down to the bass cleft space notes:

All   Cows   Eat   Grass

Finally the bass clef line notes:

Green   Buses   Drive   Fast   Always

Look at the written music as you pick out these notes on the keyboard. It takes a little time to remember the sayings but it will enable you to work out the letter names and where each note is positioned more easily.

PLAYING PIECES FROM THE STAVE

Carefully play through the next piece. Concentrate on learning the notes before you focus on the timing. (Small numbers written above or below the notes are finger numbers).

WHEN THE SAINTS GO MARCHING IN

1) * This curved line is called a tie and is connecting a semibreve, (worth 4 beats) to a crotchet.

Play the first G and hold the key down through the second G.

Altogether you wait for 5 beats.

2) * This middle C is a dotted minim and has the time value of 3 beats.

Now play these pieces with the left hand "C" position. (Little finger of left hand on the C below middle C).

L.H. MELODY IN C

MARY HAD A LITTLE LAMB

USING BOTH HANDS

When playing with two hands, make sure you place all your fingers over the correct keys. You will find that a suggested "fingering" will be indicated in most written music.

In this case: C position in R.H. (place 1st finger on middle C)

F position in L.H. (place 5th finger on F below middle C)

R.H.				1	2	3	4	5
	F	G	A	B	C	D	E	F	G
L.H.	5	4	3	2	1			

The treble and bass clef staves are used together to form one "line" of piano music.

STUDY FOR 2 HANDS

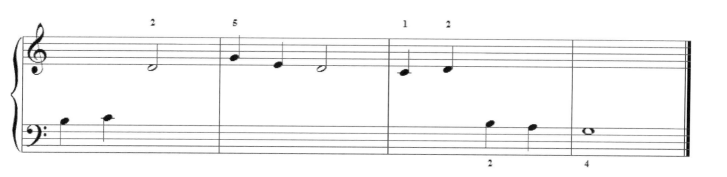

Having learnt the notes, start to count 4 beats in every bar and try to make the whole piece legato (see page 3).

Practise this next exercise for more finger independence. Try to keep an even beat, and play each note with equal "weight" and tone.

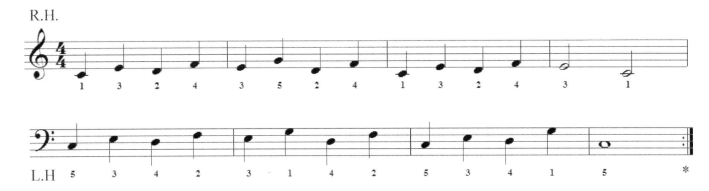

* Double dots mean repeat from the beginning.

This next piece has a time signature of $\frac{3}{4}$ (3 crotchets per bar).

Count 1, 2, 3 in every bar.

Practise slowly at first, then build up to a fairly quick tempo.

ROW, ROW, ROW YOUR BOAT

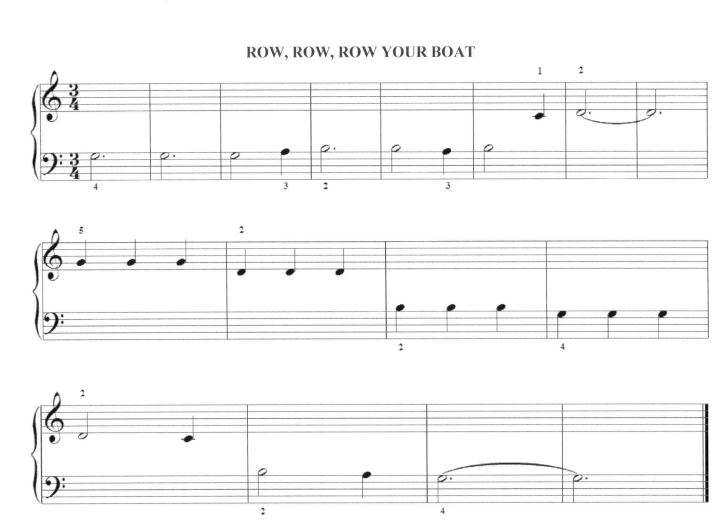

HANDS TOGETHER

Before learning English Song, play the 5-note C position hands together as shown. Keep the fingers close to the keys and make sure they are played at exactly the same time.

Note: When notes play together, they are written directly above and below each other.

Practise each hand of this song separately until you are comfortable, then carefully try hands together.

Remember to hold down the left hand semibreves for the full 4 beats of the bar.

ENGLISH SONG

Will Waitt

Stage 8 (cont.)

You need to change the R.H. position slightly in this piece by playing the first G's (notes marked with an *) with the 4th finger after the middle C's are sounded.

The last C on line one and line three are played with the 2nd finger passing over the thumb.

TWINKLE TWINKLE LITTLE STAR

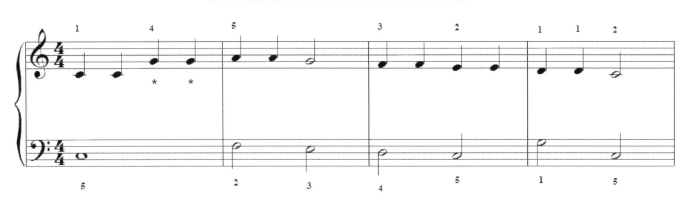

15

QUAVERS

Half beat notes are called quavers and look like this ♪ or ♫ when joined.

They are twice as fast as crotchets and can also be called eighth notes.

PEAS PUDDING HOT

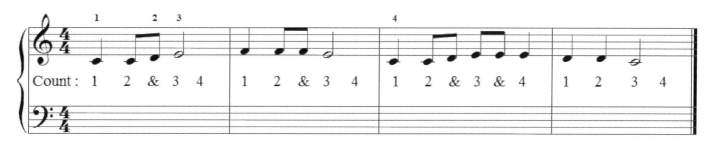

MUSETTE

* These are 1 beat rests

J.S. Bach

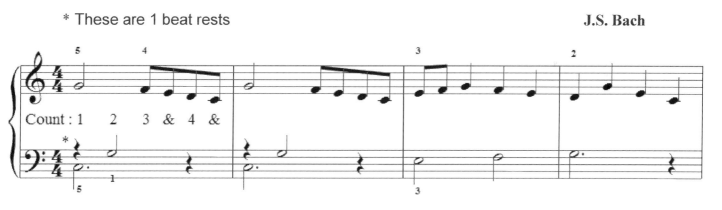

RESTS

Rests are an integral part of music and are as rhythmically important as the notes.

They can be of any time value and when you see a rest, you simply lift your finger(s) off the keys. Below are the most common examples:

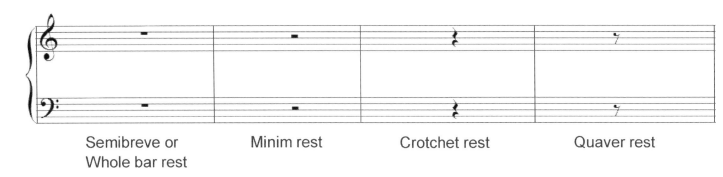

Semibreve or   Minim rest   Crotchet rest   Quaver rest
Whole bar rest

TAKE A BREATH!

Make sure you count 3 beats in every bar in the next song.

Count the rests just as you would the notes.

COUNTRY BLUES

Will Waitt

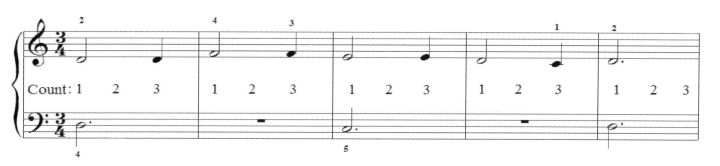

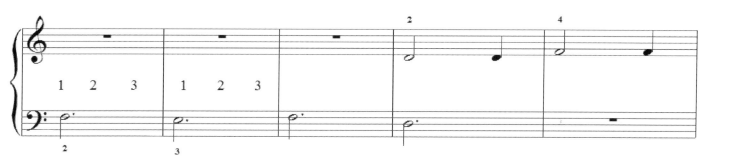

* Move hand down an octave to play this D.

BLACK KEYS

There are two different names for the black keys: Sharps and Flats.

Sharps move up one semitone, (the closest distance between two keys).

If you play an F, then F sharp would be the first in the group of three black notes.

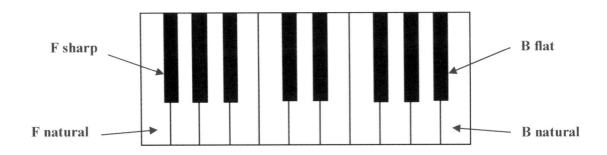

This is how sharps are written:

Flats go down one semitone from any note and look like this:

Natural signs cancel out the previous sharps or flats in the same bar and are written:

The following pieces introduce the use of sharps, flats and naturals.

Use D position in both hands: Thumb on D in right hand, (treble clef). 5th finger on D below in left hand, (bass clef).

WALTZ IN D

Will Waitt

BLUES IN C

Use C position in both hands

Will Waitt

DOTTED RHYTHMS

This next piece contains a new timing note called a dotted crotchet. It is worth 1½ beats and is often followed by a quaver (worth a ½ beat). The combined length of these two notes is 2 beats.

First try this timing exercise. When counting the dotted crotchets, say aloud 1&2 then count "and" on the remaining quaver.

Again, practise this piece hands separately first and keep notes as smooth (legato) as possible.

NEW WORLD SYMPHONY

Dvořák

Note: In most piano music, the melody of a piece is played with the right hand. The left hand plays the accompaniment. Sometimes however, the left hand takes the leading role as in this next example. Practise it a few times hands separately before trying hands together.

MELODY FOR THE LEFT HAND

Will Waitt

Count: 1 & 2 & 3 & 4 &   1 & 2 & 3 & 4 &   1 & 2 & 3 & 4 &   1 & 2 & 3 & 4 &

* To play this note B, slightly extend your thumb to the left.

SOLID AND BROKEN CHORDS

A chord normally contains 3 notes. If the letter note of the chord is the lowest note, then it is a "root" chord, i.e. the root position of C chord is C E G.

Place your R.H. fingers, 1 3 5, over these keys and play all three simultaneously (Solid Chord). Try not to bend the wrist, and only use the weight of the arm.

Then play the notes one at a time (Broken Chord).

Now play the same chord in the left hand.

Also practise the chords of F and G.

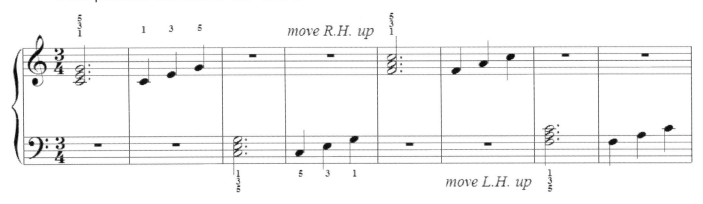

SKIP TO MY LOU

Traditional

* Lift your hand off the chords on these crotchet (1 beat) rests.

12 BAR BLUES IN C

Will Waitt

DIFFERENT HAND POSITIONS

As pieces get more difficult, your hands have to change positions more often. Just as you have been moving your hand to different places in the last two pieces, your fingers sometimes need to be spread out in a more "open" position.

Try playing the broken chord of C with this fingering in the right hand.

Then in the left hand.

Now try this same pattern in the chord of D.

Stage 14 (cont.)

These next two well-known songs contain "solid" and "broken" chords.

Learn the notes carefully hands apart, and try to put your fingers over the keys before playing them. Remember to change hand positions smoothly.

HAPPY BIRTHDAY

Anon.

* Pass your 2nd finger over your thumb.

KUM-BA YA

Traditional

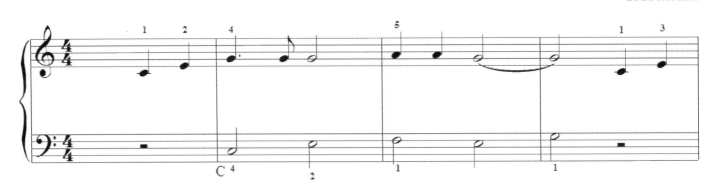

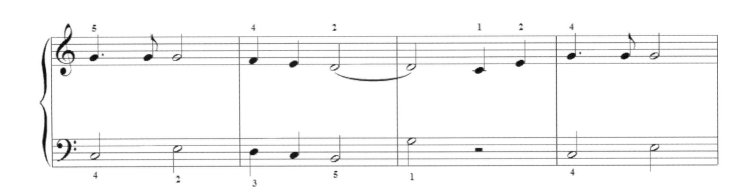

When you can play this piece hands together, try to keep the left hand quieter than the right.

SCALES AND PASSING THE THUMB UNDER

You need to get used to passing your thumb under the fingers or moving the hand over the thumb. First learn the scale of C over one octave. (Scales use all 7 letter notes).

Keep the tempo slow and even. Let the arm move the hand sideways along the keyboard and get the thumb ready early. Avoid any tension in the wrist or arm.

Practise these scales several times before learning the next 2 pieces.

THE STREAM

Will Waitt

* Pause or fermata sign. Hold these notes slightly longer than their normal value.

BOOGIE STOMP

Will Waitt

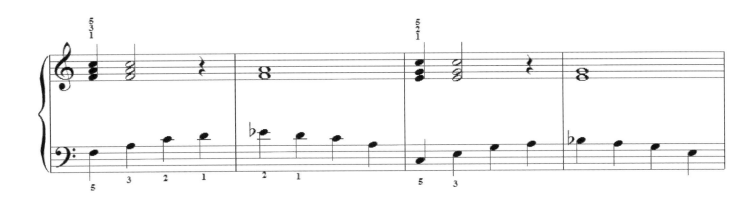

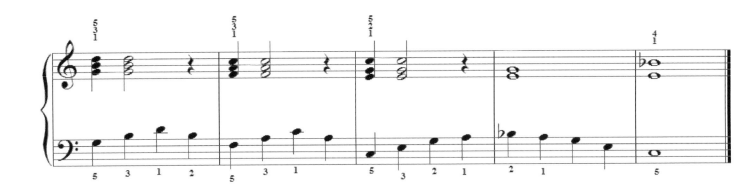

Always lift fingers off the keys on the crotchet rests. This will also help to keep the left hand legato.

THE NEW TIME SIGNATURES OF $\frac{3}{8}$ AND $\frac{6}{8}$

So far we have covered $\frac{4}{4}$ (common time), $\frac{3}{4}$ (3 crotchets per bar) and $\frac{2}{4}$ (2 crotchets a bar). The lower 4 on all these time signatures donates a crotchet or 1 note beat. However, if the lower number is an 8 as in $\frac{3}{8}$ then you have 3 quavers per bar. In $\frac{6}{8}$ there are 6 quavers per bar.

Try this timing exercise. Count 2 groups of 3 per bar.

Note: There are 2 "main" beats a bar in $\frac{6}{8}$ each worth a dotted crotchet.

MELLOW BREEZE

Will Waitt

Play the quavers in this piece as evenly as possible, and count 3 beats per bar.

SEMIQUAVERS

Semiquavers have two beams or tails and are worth half a crotchet. Individually they look like this: ♪ More often they are joined together in pairs or groups of three or four i.e.:

Another common way semiquavers are used is when a dotted quaver is followed by a semiquaver. The next two pieces mainly use this rhythm. Always give yourself enough time on the dotted quaver so the semiquaver will be quick enough.

FOLK DANCE

Will Waitt

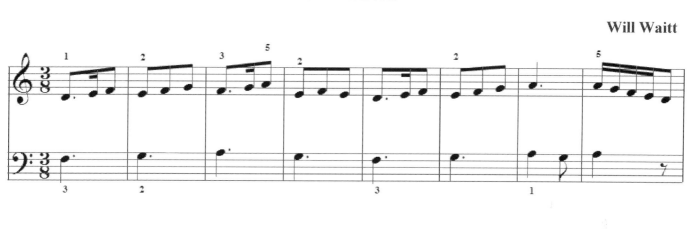

GREENSLEAVES

Traditional

Practise the right hand of this piece slowly and with the correct fingering. Make sure you are confident with the left hand before playing hands together, and try to keep the notes legato throughout.

KEY SIGNATURES AND MAJOR "KEYS"

Key signatures are sharps and flats written at the beginning of every stave. They tell you what "key" the piece is in and which notes are automatically sharpened or flattened. If only an F sharp is in the key signature then you will be in the key of G major and all the F's will be sharp.

Having a B flat in the key signature will signify you are in the key of F major. All B's are flattened.

Learn the notes of G scale first and always try for accurate fingering and good legato.

Be aware that the right hand fingering of F major scale is slightly different.

When you know the notes to this piece, try to count 2 strong beats per bar.

MARCH IN G

Will Waitt

Stage 18 (cont.)

Remember that all the B's in this piece are automatically flattened unless there is a natural sign (♮) placed before them.

* At this point, repeat from the double bar line at the beginning, then continue onto the second time bar, ** through to the end.

WILLIAM TELL THEME

Rossini

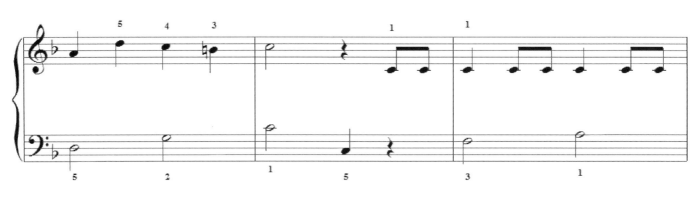

DYNAMICS

Originally the piano was called a PIANOFORTE. The "piano" meaning soft, the "forte" meaning loud. Most earlier keyboard instruments could only play at one dynamic level. By the 18th century and the advent of the piano, musicians could now enjoy the full range of the dynamics and expression no previous keyboard possessed.

By using more arm weight the hammers could strike the strings faster and therefore louder. Lighten the arms, and conversely the hammers will strike the strings more slowly and therefore make a softer sound. Practising these techniques takes time, but is really worth the effort.

These are the most common dynamic markings:

$\boldsymbol{p}$ = soft

$\boldsymbol{mp}$ = medium soft

$\boldsymbol{mf}$ = medium loud

$\boldsymbol{f}$ = loud

Use these four different "volumes" in the next exercises.

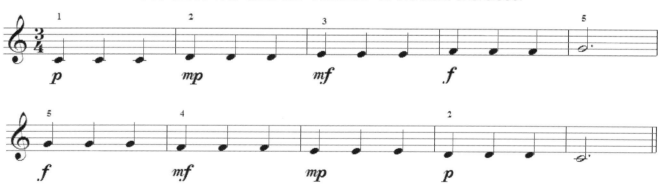

Try not to tighten up or use force when you play loud, just let the arm feel "heavier".

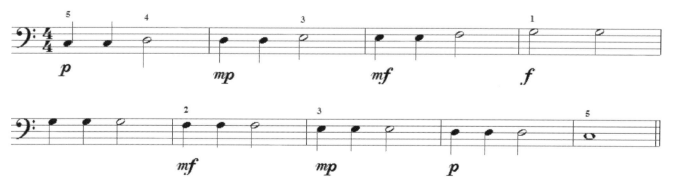

When playing soft, allow the arm to feel "lighter" but still make sure the keys go all the way down.

Learn the notes and timing of this piece without dynamics, and only start adding them in when you feel confident with your playing.

WALKIN' BLUES

Will Waitt

*1) $\frac{12}{8}$ This time signature means 12 quavers per bar. Count 123, 123, 123, 123 every bar.

*2) These lines mean gradually get louder (*crescendo*).

*3) These lines mean gradually get quieter (*diminuendo*).

CHORD INVERSIONS

Although you have already played a few different "shapes" or inversions of chords, you need to be able to move from one to another as freely as possible, and understand how they work.

Start with C major in the Right Hand.

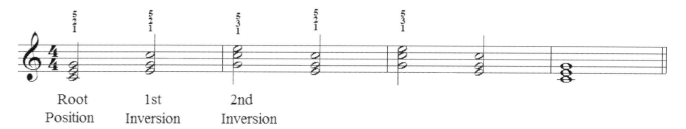

Root 1st 2nd
Position Inversion Inversion

Note: All these chords are still only made up from the notes of C major triad,
(C, E & G).

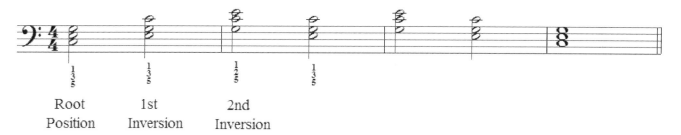

Root 1st 2nd
Position Inversion Inversion

Also practise D major, (D, F♯ & A). Play hands separately.

* The key signature of D major contains 2 sharps. F sharp and C sharp.

When changing chord shapes, move your hand along close to the keyboard and make sure the fingers touch all 3 keys before playing the chord.

THEME FROM PEER GYNT

Grieg

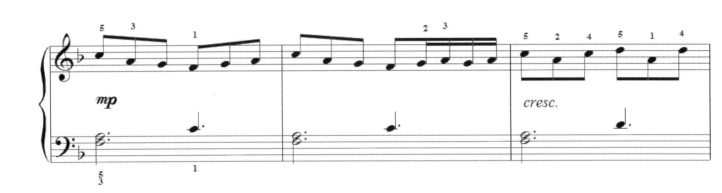

* The left hand is playing 2 "lines" or voices known as part writing.

The lower line is made up of the 2-note chords and the upper part consists of the dotted crotchets. Hold the chords for the whole bar and play the dotted crotchets after counting 3 quavers.

R.H. over

ARPEGGIOS

Arpeggios are really broken chords played over one octave or more. They usually involve the thumb passing under the fingers or the fingers passing over the thumb. (Similar to scale technique). It is important to keep the arm and wrist free and relaxed so the hand can move easily along the keyboard.

Spend some time on this exercise.

Now try C major arpeggio over 2 octaves.

Make sure the thumb passes under the hand early when ascending in R.H. and descending in L.H.

Also practise D major arpeggio.

SHERWOOD FOREST

Will Waitt

Practise slowly at first and always keep semiquavers light and even.

FÜR ELISE

Poco Moto

Beethoven

TEMPO AND METRONOME MARKINGS

Most pieces or songs have a written instruction at the beginning to indicate the approximate speed or tempo. Italian words are usually used.

For example: **Moderato** – at a moderate pace

Andante – at a walking pace

Largo – slowly

To play the music at an exact speed composers or editors sometimes give a metronome marking, i.e. ♩ = 100. This means 100 crotchets per minute.

Likewise, ♩ = 60 is 60 minims per minute.

Always treat these markings as a guide rather than set in stone!

Metronomes are very useful to help you develop a steady pulse or beat.

Get to know the notes of a piece as well as possible before playing along with a metronome. Don't worry if you go out of time at first, maintaining an accurate and steady tempo takes a good deal of practice.

Start by first playing this next piece **largo** then build up to **moderato.**

PIANO SONG

♩ = 84 to ♩ = 138

Will Wait

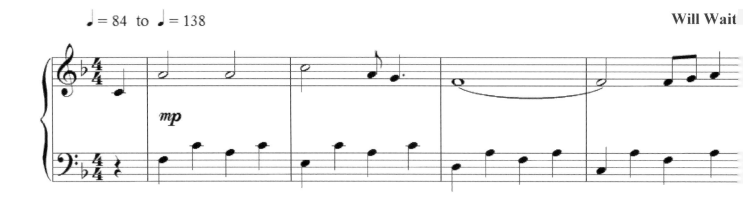

* **rit. (ritardando)** – gradually slow down.

MINOR KEYS AND CHORDS

Although we have already used minor chords and have played some pieces in minor keys (e.g. Für Elise), it is important to know the difference in sound between major and minor and how the changes are made.

With root position triads, (3-note chords), the middle note of the major chord drops a semi-tone to form the minor triad:

The difference between a major and minor 'key' can be demonstrated by looking at a complete scale.

D major would be written like this:

D minor like this:

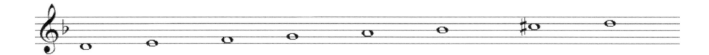

Note: Apart from the key-signatures being different, the main change in sound is caused by the 3rd and 6th notes of the scale being lowered or flattened by one semitone. Therefore F sharp and B natural in the major key become F natural and B flat in the minor.

These next two pieces sound quite different only because the first is in D major and the second in D minor. All the timing and 'letter notes' are identical. Practise both carefully and listen to the changes between them.

SERENADE IN D (MAJOR)

* Moderato

Will Waitt

* At a moderate speed

SERENADE IN D (MINOR)

Andante

Will Waitt

STACCATO AND PHRASING

Staccato is the opposite of legato. Play the notes detached as opposed to joined or smooth. A dot above or below the note indicates staccato. In C position, play the five fingers ascending and descending. Spring off each key using the wrist, and allow the hand to "drop" back to the keyboard ready for the next finger to play.

Putting in phrase marks is a way of dividing pieces into musical "sentences", just as commas and full stops are used in writing, in music curved lines are added. They can cover just a few notes or many bars.

2 and 4 bar phrases are very common, i.e.

A singer or woodwind player would generally breathe at the end of each phrase. In piano music you can lift your fingers off the keys if there are no rests, just before starting the next phrase. However, there is no single "rule" for phrasing, it is something you develop over time.

Carefully practise this next piece. Play hands separately and slowly at first before gradually putting them together. When you feel reasonably confident you can add in the dynamics and staccato.

MINUET IN G

J. S. Bach

SYNCOPATED RHYTHM

Syncopation is playing notes "offbeat", or between the main beats. Try this exercise keeping the L.H. rhythm very steady. Then add in the R.H. and play slightly louder on the accented notes.

Rag time, (most notably Scott Joplin) exploited this type of syncopation. Although his original piano scores are difficult, I'm sure you can, (with some patient practice) learn this version.

THE ENTERTAINER

Scott Joplin

Not Fast

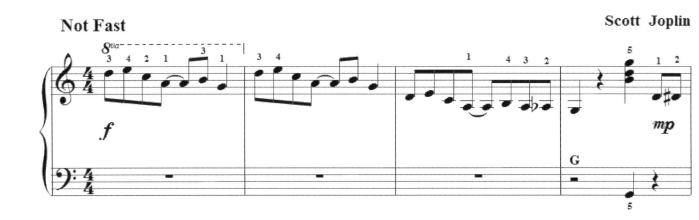

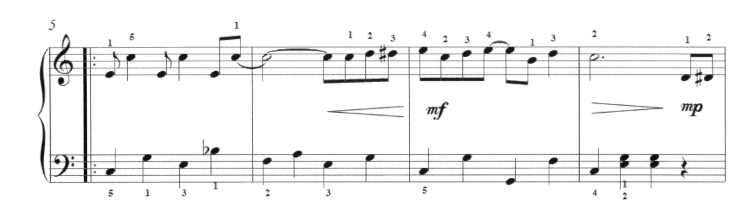

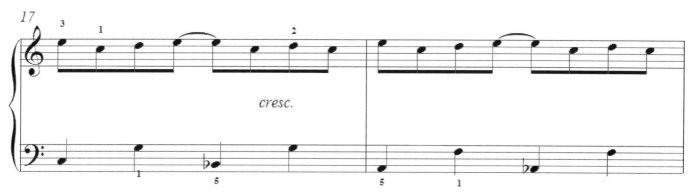

AUTHORS NOTE: Having successfully completed this book you now have the knowledge and basic skills to learn more advanced and varied piano music.

By practising daily you will soon reap the rewards and improve both your technique and overall musicality.

Printed in Great Britain
by Amazon